SERMON NOTES

*C*APTURE THE WORD.

*R*EFLECT ON THE MESSAGE.

*W*ALK IN FAITH.

Atosha Logan

SERMON NOTES

CAPTURE THE WORD.
REFLECT ON THE MESSAGE.
WALK IN FAITH.

Atosha Logan

FOR PERMISSION REQUESTS, CONTACT THE AUTHOR AT:
ATOSHA LOGAN, AUTHOR & PUBLISHER
INFO@ATOSHALOGAN.COM
WWW.ATOSHALOGAN.COM

ISBN:979-8-9931753-2-4 (PAPERBACK)

PRINTED IN THE UNITED STATES OF AMERICA

COVER DESIGN: ATOSHA LOGAN
INTERIOR LAYOUT: ATOSHA LOGAN

Welcome to your Sermon Notes Journal

— a sacred space to *capture* the truths of God's Word, *reflect* on His message, and *walk* in faith.

This journal is designed to help you listen with purpose, write with clarity, and live with obedience. Each page is an invitation to draw nearer to God through His Word and to be transformed by it.

Capture the Word

"Write the vision; make it plain on tablets, so he may run who reads it." — *Habakkuk 2:2 (ESV)*

God's Word is living and active. As you take notes, you are preserving His truth so it can take root in your heart and guide your steps.

Reflect on the Message

"But his delight is in the law of the Lord, and on his law he meditates day and night." — *Psalm 1:2 (ESV)*

Reflection turns hearing into understanding. Meditating on scripture and sermons allows God's Word to shape your mind, renew your spirit, and deepen your walk.

Walk in Faith

"For we walk by faith, not by sight." — *2 Corinthians 5:7*
"But be doers of the word, and not hearers only, deceiving yourselves." — *James 1:22 (ESV)*

Faith grows when the Word is put into action. As you apply what you've written and reflected upon, you'll see God's promises unfold in your life.

May this journal be a faithful companion on your journey — reminding you to capture God's Word, reflect deeply on His truth, and walk daily in faith.

This Book
belongs to:

_____

_____

_____

SERMON NOTES

DATE:

SPEAKER

TOPIC

SCRIPTURE REFERENCE(S)

o

o

o

o

KEY POINTS

NOTES

CAPTURE THE WORD	REFLECT ON THE MESSAGE	WALK IN FAITH

SERMON NOTES

DATE:

SPEAKER   **TOPIC**

SCRIPTURE REFERENCE(S)

- o
- o
- o
- o

KEY POINTS

NOTES

CAPTURE THE WORD	REFLECT ON THE MESSAGE	WALK IN FAITH

SERMON NOTES

DATE:

SPEAKER

TOPIC

SCRIPTURE REFERENCE(S)

o

o

o

o

KEY POINTS

NOTES

CAPTURE THE WORD	REFLECT ON THE MESSAGE	WALK IN FAITH

SERMON NOTES

DATE:

SPEAKER   **TOPIC**

SCRIPTURE REFERENCE(S)

-
-
-
-

KEY POINTS

NOTES

CAPTURE THE WORD	REFLECT ON THE MESSAGE	WALK IN FAITH

SERMON NOTES

DATE:

SPEAKER   **TOPIC**

SCRIPTURE REFERENCE(S)

- o
- o
- o
- o

KEY POINTS

NOTES

CAPTURE THE WORD	REFLECT ON THE MESSAGE	WALK IN FAITH

SERMON NOTES

DATE:

SPEAKER   **TOPIC**

SCRIPTURE REFERENCE(S)

- o
- o
- o
- o

KEY POINTS

NOTES

CAPTURE THE WORD	REFLECT ON THE MESSAGE	WALK IN FAITH

SERMON NOTES

DATE:

SPEAKER   **TOPIC**

SCRIPTURE REFERENCE(S)

o

o

o

o

KEY POINTS

NOTES

CAPTURE THE WORD	REFLECT ON THE MESSAGE	WALK IN FAITH

SERMON
NOTES

DATE:

SPEAKER   **TOPIC**

SCRIPTURE REFERENCE(S)

○

○

○

○

KEY POINTS

NOTES

CAPTURE THE WORD	REFLECT ON THE MESSAGE	WALK IN FAITH

SERMON
NOTES

DATE:

SPEAKER   **TOPIC**

SCRIPTURE REFERENCE(S)

o
o
o
o

KEY POINTS

NOTES

_____

_____

_____

_____

_____

_____

_____

_____

_____

_____

_____

_____

_____

_____

_____

CAPTURE THE WORD	REFLECT ON THE MESSAGE	WALK IN FAITH

SERMON
NOTES

DATE:

SPEAKER   **TOPIC**

SCRIPTURE REFERENCE(S)

o

o

o

o

KEY POINTS

NOTES

CAPTURE THE WORD	REFLECT ON THE MESSAGE	WALK IN FAITH

SERMON NOTES

DATE:

SPEAKER   **TOPIC**

SCRIPTURE REFERENCE(S)

o

o

o

o

KEY POINTS

NOTES

CAPTURE THE WORD	REFLECT ON THE MESSAGE	WALK IN FAITH

SERMON NOTES

DATE:

SPEAKER   **TOPIC**

SCRIPTURE REFERENCE(S)

o
o
o
o

KEY POINTS

NOTES

CAPTURE THE WORD	REFLECT ON THE MESSAGE	WALK IN FAITH

SERMON
NOTES

DATE:

SPEAKER   **TOPIC**

SCRIPTURE REFERENCE(S)

○

○

○

○

KEY POINTS

NOTES

CAPTURE THE WORD	REFLECT ON THE MESSAGE	WALK IN FAITH

SERMON
NOTES

DATE:

SPEAKER   **TOPIC**

SCRIPTURE REFERENCE(S)

o

o

o

o

KEY POINTS

NOTES

CAPTURE THE WORD	REFLECT ON THE MESSAGE	WALK IN FAITH

SERMON
NOTES

DATE:

SPEAKER   **TOPIC**

SCRIPTURE REFERENCE(S)

o

o

o

o

KEY POINTS

NOTES

CAPTURE THE WORD	REFLECT ON THE MESSAGE	WALK IN FAITH

SERMON
NOTES

DATE:

SPEAKER   **TOPIC**

SCRIPTURE REFERENCE(S)

○

○

○

○

KEY POINTS

NOTES

CAPTURE THE WORD	REFLECT ON THE MESSAGE	WALK IN FAITH

SERMON NOTES

DATE:

SPEAKER

TOPIC

SCRIPTURE REFERENCE(S)

o

o

o

o

KEY POINTS

NOTES

CAPTURE THE WORD	REFLECT ON THE MESSAGE	WALK IN FAITH

SERMON NOTES

DATE:

SPEAKER   **TOPIC**

SCRIPTURE REFERENCE(S)

o

o

o

o

KEY POINTS

NOTES

CAPTURE THE WORD	REFLECT ON THE MESSAGE	WALK IN FAITH

SERMON NOTES

DATE:

SPEAKER   **TOPIC**

SCRIPTURE REFERENCE(S)

o

o

o

o

KEY POINTS

_____

_____

_____

_____

_____

_____

_____

_____

_____

NOTES

CAPTURE THE WORD	REFLECT ON THE MESSAGE	WALK IN FAITH

SERMON
NOTES

DATE:

SPEAKER   **TOPIC**

SCRIPTURE REFERENCE(S)

o

o

o

o

KEY POINTS

NOTES

CAPTURE THE WORD	REFLECT ON THE MESSAGE	WALK IN FAITH

SERMON NOTES

DATE:

SPEAKER   **TOPIC**

SCRIPTURE REFERENCE(S)

o

o

o

o

KEY POINTS

NOTES

CAPTURE THE WORD	REFLECT ON THE MESSAGE	WALK IN FAITH

SERMON NOTES

DATE:

SPEAKER   **TOPIC**

SCRIPTURE REFERENCE(S)

o
o
o
o

KEY POINTS

NOTES

CAPTURE THE WORD	REFLECT ON THE MESSAGE	WALK IN FAITH

SERMON
NOTES

DATE:

SPEAKER **TOPIC**

SCRIPTURE REFERENCE(S)

- o
- o
- o
- o

KEY POINTS

_____
_____
_____
_____
_____
_____
_____
_____

NOTES

CAPTURE THE WORD	REFLECT ON THE MESSAGE	WALK IN FAITH

SERMON NOTES

DATE:

SPEAKER   **TOPIC**

SCRIPTURE REFERENCE(S)

o

o

o

o

KEY POINTS

NOTES

CAPTURE THE WORD	REFLECT ON THE MESSAGE	WALK IN FAITH

SERMON NOTES

DATE:

SPEAKER   **TOPIC**

SCRIPTURE REFERENCE(S)

o

o

o

o

KEY POINTS

NOTES

CAPTURE THE WORD	REFLECT ON THE MESSAGE	WALK IN FAITH

SERMON NOTES

DATE:

SPEAKER   **TOPIC**

SCRIPTURE REFERENCE(S)

o

o

o

o

KEY POINTS

NOTES

CAPTURE THE WORD	REFLECT ON THE MESSAGE	WALK IN FAITH

SERMON NOTES

DATE:

SPEAKER   **TOPIC**

SCRIPTURE REFERENCE(S)

o

o

o

o

KEY POINTS

CAPTURE THE WORD	REFLECT ON THE MESSAGE	WALK IN FAITH

SERMON NOTES

DATE:

SPEAKER   **TOPIC**

SCRIPTURE REFERENCE(S)

- ○
- ○
- ○
- ○

KEY POINTS

NOTES

_____
_____
_____
_____
_____
_____
_____
_____
_____
_____
_____
_____
_____
_____
_____

CAPTURE THE WORD	REFLECT ON THE MESSAGE	WALK IN FAITH

SERMON NOTES

DATE:

SPEAKER   **TOPIC**

SCRIPTURE REFERENCE(S)

o

o

o

o

KEY POINTS

NOTES

CAPTURE THE WORD	REFLECT ON THE MESSAGE	WALK IN FAITH

SERMON
NOTES

DATE:

SPEAKER   **TOPIC**

SCRIPTURE REFERENCE(S)

o

o

o

o

KEY POINTS

NOTES

CAPTURE THE WORD	REFLECT ON THE MESSAGE	WALK IN FAITH

SERMON NOTES

DATE:

SPEAKER   **TOPIC**

SCRIPTURE REFERENCE(S)

- ○
- ○
- ○
- ○

KEY POINTS

CAPTURE THE WORD	REFLECT ON THE MESSAGE	WALK IN FAITH

SERMON
NOTES

DATE:

SPEAKER   **TOPIC**

SCRIPTURE REFERENCE(S)

o

o

o

o

KEY POINTS

NOTES

CAPTURE THE WORD	REFLECT ON THE MESSAGE	WALK IN FAITH

SERMON
NOTES

DATE:

SPEAKER   **TOPIC**

SCRIPTURE REFERENCE(S)

o

o

o

o

KEY POINTS

NOTES

CAPTURE THE WORD	REFLECT ON THE MESSAGE	WALK IN FAITH

SERMON
NOTES

DATE:

SPEAKER   **TOPIC**

SCRIPTURE REFERENCE(S)

○

○

○

○

KEY POINTS

CAPTURE THE WORD	REFLECT ON THE MESSAGE	WALK IN FAITH

SERMON
NOTES

DATE:

SPEAKER   **TOPIC**

SCRIPTURE REFERENCE(S)

o

o

o

o

KEY POINTS

_____
_____
_____
_____
_____
_____
_____
_____
_____

NOTES

_____
_____
_____
_____
_____
_____
_____
_____
_____
_____
_____
_____
_____
_____

CAPTURE THE WORD	REFLECT ON THE MESSAGE	WALK IN FAITH

SERMON NOTES

DATE:

SPEAKER   **TOPIC**

SCRIPTURE REFERENCE(S)

o

o

o

o

KEY POINTS

_____

_____

_____

_____

_____

_____

_____

_____

_____

NOTES

CAPTURE THE WORD	REFLECT ON THE MESSAGE	WALK IN FAITH

SERMON
NOTES

DATE:

SPEAKER   **TOPIC**

SCRIPTURE REFERENCE(S)

o

o

o

o

KEY POINTS

NOTES

CAPTURE THE WORD	REFLECT ON THE MESSAGE	WALK IN FAITH

SERMON
NOTES

DATE:

SPEAKER   **TOPIC**

SCRIPTURE REFERENCE(S)

o

o

o

o

KEY POINTS

NOTES

CAPTURE THE WORD	REFLECT ON THE MESSAGE	WALK IN FAITH

SERMON NOTES

DATE:

SPEAKER   **TOPIC**

SCRIPTURE REFERENCE(S)

o

o

o

o

KEY POINTS

NOTES

CAPTURE THE WORD	REFLECT ON THE MESSAGE	WALK IN FAITH

SERMON
NOTES

DATE:

SPEAKER   **TOPIC**

SCRIPTURE REFERENCE(S)

o

o

o

o

KEY POINTS

NOTES

_____
_____
_____
_____
_____
_____
_____
_____
_____
_____
_____
_____
_____
_____
_____

CAPTURE THE WORD	REFLECT ON THE MESSAGE	WALK IN FAITH

SERMON
NOTES

DATE:

SPEAKER   **TOPIC**

SCRIPTURE REFERENCE(S)

o

o

o

o

KEY POINTS

NOTES

CAPTURE THE WORD	REFLECT ON THE MESSAGE	WALK IN FAITH

SERMON
NOTES

DATE:

SPEAKER   **TOPIC**

SCRIPTURE REFERENCE(S)

o

o

o

o

KEY POINTS

NOTES

CAPTURE THE WORD	REFLECT ON THE MESSAGE	WALK IN FAITH

SERMON NOTES

DATE:

SPEAKER   **TOPIC**

SCRIPTURE REFERENCE(S)

- ○
- ○
- ○
- ○

KEY POINTS

_____

_____

_____

_____

_____

_____

_____

_____

_____

_____

NOTES

_____
_____
_____
_____
_____
_____
_____
_____
_____
_____
_____
_____
_____
_____
_____

CAPTURE THE WORD	REFLECT ON THE MESSAGE	WALK IN FAITH

SERMON
NOTES

DATE:

SPEAKER   **TOPIC**

SCRIPTURE REFERENCE(S)

o

o

o

o

KEY POINTS

NOTES

CAPTURE THE WORD	REFLECT ON THE MESSAGE	WALK IN FAITH

SERMON NOTES

DATE:

SPEAKER   **TOPIC**

SCRIPTURE REFERENCE(S)

o
o
o
o

KEY POINTS

_____
_____
_____
_____
_____
_____
_____
_____
_____

NOTES

CAPTURE THE WORD	REFLECT ON THE MESSAGE	WALK IN FAITH

SERMON NOTES

DATE:

SPEAKER   **TOPIC**

SCRIPTURE REFERENCE(S)

○

○

○

○

KEY POINTS

NOTES

_____
_____
_____
_____
_____
_____
_____
_____
_____
_____
_____
_____
_____
_____
_____
_____

CAPTURE THE WORD	REFLECT ON THE MESSAGE	WALK IN FAITH

SERMON NOTES

DATE:

SPEAKER　　　　　　　　**TOPIC**

SCRIPTURE REFERENCE(S)

o

o

o

o

KEY POINTS

NOTES

CAPTURE THE WORD	REFLECT ON THE MESSAGE	WALK IN FAITH

SERMON
NOTES

DATE:

SPEAKER   **TOPIC**

SCRIPTURE REFERENCE(S)

o
o
o
o

KEY POINTS

NOTES

_____
_____
_____
_____
_____
_____
_____
_____
_____
_____
_____
_____
_____
_____
_____

CAPTURE THE WORD	REFLECT ON THE MESSAGE	WALK IN FAITH

SERMON NOTES

DATE:

SPEAKER   **TOPIC**

SCRIPTURE REFERENCE(S)

o

o

o

o

KEY POINTS

NOTES

CAPTURE THE WORD	REFLECT ON THE MESSAGE	WALK IN FAITH

SERMON
NOTES

DATE:

SPEAKER   **TOPIC**

SCRIPTURE REFERENCE(S)

o

o

o

o

KEY POINTS

NOTES

CAPTURE THE WORD	REFLECT ON THE MESSAGE	WALK IN FAITH

SERMON NOTES

DATE:

SPEAKER   **TOPIC**

SCRIPTURE REFERENCE(S)

o

o

o

o

KEY POINTS

NOTES

CAPTURE THE WORD	REFLECT ON THE MESSAGE	WALK IN FAITH

SERMON NOTES

DATE:

SPEAKER   **TOPIC**

SCRIPTURE REFERENCE(S)

o

o

o

o

KEY POINTS

NOTES

CAPTURE THE WORD	REFLECT ON THE MESSAGE	WALK IN FAITH

SERMON
NOTES

DATE:

SPEAKER   **TOPIC**

SCRIPTURE REFERENCE(S)

o

o

o

o

KEY POINTS

NOTES

_____
_____
_____
_____
_____
_____
_____
_____
_____
_____
_____
_____
_____
_____
_____

CAPTURE THE WORD	REFLECT ON THE MESSAGE	WALK IN FAITH

SERMON
NOTES

DATE:

SPEAKER   **TOPIC**

SCRIPTURE REFERENCE(S)

○

○

○

○

KEY POINTS

_____

_____

_____

_____

_____

_____

_____

_____

_____

NOTES

CAPTURE THE WORD	REFLECT ON THE MESSAGE	WALK IN FAITH

SERMON NOTES

DATE:

SPEAKER   **TOPIC**

SCRIPTURE REFERENCE(S)

- ○
- ○
- ○
- ○

KEY POINTS

_____
_____
_____
_____
_____
_____
_____
_____
_____

NOTES

CAPTURE THE WORD	REFLECT ON THE MESSAGE	WALK IN FAITH

SERMON NOTES

DATE:

SPEAKER

TOPIC

SCRIPTURE REFERENCE(S)

- ○
- ○
- ○
- ○

KEY POINTS

_____
_____
_____
_____
_____
_____
_____
_____
_____

NOTES

CAPTURE THE WORD	REFLECT ON THE MESSAGE	WALK IN FAITH

SERMON NOTES

DATE:

SPEAKER   **TOPIC**

SCRIPTURE REFERENCE(S)

o

o

o

o

KEY POINTS

NOTES

CAPTURE THE WORD	REFLECT ON THE MESSAGE	WALK IN FAITH

SERMON NOTES

DATE:

SPEAKER

TOPIC

SCRIPTURE REFERENCE(S)

- ○
- ○
- ○
- ○

KEY POINTS

_____

_____

_____

_____

_____

_____

_____

_____

NOTES

CAPTURE THE WORD	REFLECT ON THE MESSAGE	WALK IN FAITH

SERMON
NOTES

DATE:

SPEAKER   **TOPIC**

SCRIPTURE REFERENCE(S)

o

o

o

o

KEY POINTS

NOTES

CAPTURE THE WORD	REFLECT ON THE MESSAGE	WALK IN FAITH

SERMON NOTES

DATE:

SPEAKER　　　　　　　　　　**TOPIC**

SCRIPTURE REFERENCE(S)

o

o

o

o

KEY POINTS

NOTES

CAPTURE THE WORD	REFLECT ON THE MESSAGE	WALK IN FAITH

SERMON
NOTES

DATE:

SPEAKER   **TOPIC**

SCRIPTURE REFERENCE(S)

- ○
- ○
- ○
- ○

KEY POINTS

NOTES

_____

_____

_____

_____

_____

_____

_____

_____

_____

_____

_____

_____

_____

_____

_____

_____

CAPTURE THE WORD	REFLECT ON THE MESSAGE	WALK IN FAITH

SERMON
NOTES

DATE:

SPEAKER   **TOPIC**

SCRIPTURE REFERENCE(S)

-
-
-
-

KEY POINTS

NOTES

CAPTURE THE WORD	REFLECT ON THE MESSAGE	WALK IN FAITH

SERMON
NOTES

DATE:

SPEAKER   **TOPIC**

SCRIPTURE REFERENCE(S)

o

o

o

o

KEY POINTS

NOTES

_____
_____
_____
_____
_____
_____
_____
_____
_____
_____
_____
_____
_____
_____
_____
_____

CAPTURE THE WORD	REFLECT ON THE MESSAGE	WALK IN FAITH

SERMON NOTES

DATE:

SPEAKER   **TOPIC**

SCRIPTURE REFERENCE(S)

- ○
- ○
- ○
- ○

KEY POINTS

_____
_____
_____
_____
_____
_____
_____
_____
_____

NOTES

CAPTURE THE WORD	REFLECT ON THE MESSAGE	WALK IN FAITH

SERMON NOTES

DATE:

SPEAKER   **TOPIC**

SCRIPTURE REFERENCE(S)

○

○

○

○

KEY POINTS

NOTES

CAPTURE THE WORD	REFLECT ON THE MESSAGE	WALK IN FAITH

SERMON NOTES

DATE:

SPEAKER   **TOPIC**

SCRIPTURE REFERENCE(S)

o
o
o
o

KEY POINTS

NOTES

_____
_____
_____
_____
_____
_____
_____
_____
_____
_____
_____
_____
_____
_____
_____
_____

CAPTURE THE WORD	REFLECT ON THE MESSAGE	WALK IN FAITH

SERMON
NOTES

DATE:

SPEAKER   **TOPIC**

SCRIPTURE REFERENCE(S)

○

○

○

○

KEY POINTS

NOTES

CAPTURE THE WORD	REFLECT ON THE MESSAGE	WALK IN FAITH

SERMON NOTES

DATE:

SPEAKER   **TOPIC**

SCRIPTURE REFERENCE(S)

o

o

o

o

KEY POINTS

NOTES

CAPTURE THE WORD	REFLECT ON THE MESSAGE	WALK IN FAITH

SERMON NOTES

DATE:

SPEAKER   **TOPIC**

SCRIPTURE REFERENCE(S)

o

o

o

o

KEY POINTS

NOTES

CAPTURE THE WORD	REFLECT ON THE MESSAGE	WALK IN FAITH

SERMON
NOTES

DATE:

SPEAKER   **TOPIC**

SCRIPTURE REFERENCE(S)

- ○
- ○
- ○
- ○

KEY POINTS

NOTES

CAPTURE THE WORD	REFLECT ON THE MESSAGE	WALK IN FAITH

SERMON NOTES

DATE:

SPEAKER **TOPIC**

SCRIPTURE REFERENCE(S)

- ○
- ○
- ○
- ○

KEY POINTS

NOTES

CAPTURE THE WORD	REFLECT ON THE MESSAGE	WALK IN FAITH

SERMON
NOTES

DATE:

SPEAKER   **TOPIC**

SCRIPTURE REFERENCE(S)

o

o

o

o

KEY POINTS

NOTES

CAPTURE THE WORD	REFLECT ON THE MESSAGE	WALK IN FAITH

SERMON NOTES

DATE:

SPEAKER   **TOPIC**

SCRIPTURE REFERENCE(S)

o

o

o

o

KEY POINTS

NOTES

CAPTURE THE WORD	REFLECT ON THE MESSAGE	WALK IN FAITH

SERMON NOTES

DATE:

SPEAKER   **TOPIC**

SCRIPTURE REFERENCE(S)

o

o

o

o

KEY POINTS

NOTES

CAPTURE THE WORD	REFLECT ON THE MESSAGE	WALK IN FAITH

SERMON NOTES

DATE:

SPEAKER   **TOPIC**

SCRIPTURE REFERENCE(S)

○

○

○

○

KEY POINTS

_____

_____

_____

_____

_____

_____

_____

_____

_____

NOTES

CAPTURE THE WORD	REFLECT ON THE MESSAGE	WALK IN FAITH

SERMON NOTES

DATE:

SPEAKER   **TOPIC**

SCRIPTURE REFERENCE(S)

○

○

○

○

KEY POINTS

NOTES

CAPTURE THE WORD	REFLECT ON THE MESSAGE	WALK IN FAITH

SERMON NOTES

DATE:

SPEAKER   **TOPIC**

SCRIPTURE REFERENCE(S)

o

o

o

o

KEY POINTS

_____

_____

_____

_____

_____

_____

_____

_____

_____

NOTES

CAPTURE THE WORD	REFLECT ON THE MESSAGE	WALK IN FAITH

SERMON NOTES

DATE:

SPEAKER   **TOPIC**

SCRIPTURE REFERENCE(S)

o

o

o

o

KEY POINTS

NOTES

CAPTURE THE WORD	REFLECT ON THE MESSAGE	WALK IN FAITH

SERMON NOTES

DATE:

SPEAKER   **TOPIC**

SCRIPTURE REFERENCE(S)

o

o

o

o

KEY POINTS

NOTES

_____
_____
_____
_____
_____
_____
_____
_____
_____
_____
_____
_____
_____
_____
_____
_____

CAPTURE THE WORD	REFLECT ON THE MESSAGE	WALK IN FAITH

SERMON
NOTES

DATE:

SPEAKER **TOPIC**

SCRIPTURE REFERENCE(S)

- o
- o
- o
- o

KEY POINTS

_____

_____

_____

_____

_____

_____

_____

_____

_____

NOTES

_____

_____

_____

_____

_____

_____

_____

_____

_____

_____

_____

_____

_____

_____

_____

CAPTURE THE WORD	REFLECT ON THE MESSAGE	WALK IN FAITH

SERMON NOTES

DATE:

SPEAKER   **TOPIC**

SCRIPTURE REFERENCE(S)

○

○

○

○

KEY POINTS

_____

_____

_____

_____

_____

_____

_____

_____

_____

NOTES

CAPTURE THE WORD	REFLECT ON THE MESSAGE	WALK IN FAITH

SERMON
NOTES

DATE:

SPEAKER   **TOPIC**

SCRIPTURE REFERENCE(S)

- ○
- ○
- ○
- ○

KEY POINTS

_____

_____

_____

_____

_____

_____

_____

_____

_____

NOTES

CAPTURE THE WORD	REFLECT ON THE MESSAGE	WALK IN FAITH

SERMON NOTES

DATE:

SPEAKER   **TOPIC**

SCRIPTURE REFERENCE(S)

o

o

o

o

KEY POINTS

NOTES

CAPTURE THE WORD	REFLECT ON THE MESSAGE	WALK IN FAITH

SERMON NOTES

DATE:

SPEAKER   **TOPIC**

SCRIPTURE REFERENCE(S)

o

o

o

o

KEY POINTS

NOTES

_____
_____
_____
_____
_____
_____
_____
_____
_____
_____
_____
_____
_____
_____

CAPTURE THE WORD	REFLECT ON THE MESSAGE	WALK IN FAITH

SERMON NOTES

DATE:

SPEAKER   **TOPIC**

SCRIPTURE REFERENCE(S)

- ○
- ○
- ○
- ○

KEY POINTS

NOTES

CAPTURE THE WORD	REFLECT ON THE MESSAGE	WALK IN FAITH

SERMON NOTES

DATE:

SPEAKER

TOPIC

SCRIPTURE REFERENCE(S)

o

o

o

o

KEY POINTS

NOTES

CAPTURE THE WORD	REFLECT ON THE MESSAGE	WALK IN FAITH

SERMON NOTES

DATE:

SPEAKER   **TOPIC**

SCRIPTURE REFERENCE(S)

o

o

o

o

KEY POINTS

NOTES

CAPTURE THE WORD	REFLECT ON THE MESSAGE	WALK IN FAITH

SERMON
NOTES

DATE:

SPEAKER   **TOPIC**

SCRIPTURE REFERENCE(S)

○

○

○

○

KEY POINTS

_____

_____

_____

_____

_____

_____

_____

_____

_____

_____

_____

_____

_____

_____

CAPTURE THE WORD	REFLECT ON THE MESSAGE	WALK IN FAITH

SERMON
NOTES

DATE:

SPEAKER   **TOPIC**

SCRIPTURE REFERENCE(S)

o

o

o

o

KEY POINTS

NOTES

CAPTURE THE WORD	REFLECT ON THE MESSAGE	WALK IN FAITH

SERMON NOTES

DATE:

SPEAKER **TOPIC**

SCRIPTURE REFERENCE(S)

o

o

o

o

KEY POINTS

NOTES

_____
_____
_____
_____
_____
_____
_____
_____
_____
_____
_____
_____
_____
_____
_____
_____
_____

CAPTURE THE WORD	REFLECT ON THE MESSAGE	WALK IN FAITH

SERMON
NOTES

DATE:

SPEAKER   **TOPIC**

SCRIPTURE REFERENCE(S)

○

○

○

○

KEY POINTS

_____
_____
_____
_____
_____
_____
_____
_____
_____

NOTES

CAPTURE THE WORD	REFLECT ON THE MESSAGE	WALK IN FAITH

SERMON NOTES

DATE:

SPEAKER

TOPIC

SCRIPTURE REFERENCE(S)

o

o

o

o

KEY POINTS

NOTES

CAPTURE THE WORD	REFLECT ON THE MESSAGE	WALK IN FAITH

SERMON
NOTES

DATE:

SPEAKER   **TOPIC**

SCRIPTURE REFERENCE(S)

o

o

o

o

KEY POINTS

_____

_____

_____

_____

_____

_____

_____

_____

_____

NOTES

CAPTURE THE WORD	REFLECT ON THE MESSAGE	WALK IN FAITH

SERMON NOTES

DATE:

SPEAKER   **TOPIC**

SCRIPTURE REFERENCE(S)

- o
- o
- o
- o

KEY POINTS

NOTES

CAPTURE THE WORD	REFLECT ON THE MESSAGE	WALK IN FAITH

SERMON NOTES

DATE:

SPEAKER   **TOPIC**

SCRIPTURE REFERENCE(S)

-
-
-
-

KEY POINTS

NOTES

CAPTURE THE WORD	REFLECT ON THE MESSAGE	WALK IN FAITH

SERMON NOTES

DATE:

SPEAKER   **TOPIC**

SCRIPTURE REFERENCE(S)

o

o

o

o

KEY POINTS

_____

_____

_____

_____

_____

_____

_____

_____

_____

NOTES

CAPTURE THE WORD	REFLECT ON THE MESSAGE	WALK IN FAITH

SERMON NOTES

DATE:

SPEAKER   **TOPIC**

SCRIPTURE REFERENCE(S)

o
o
o
o

KEY POINTS

_____
_____
_____
_____
_____
_____
_____
_____
_____

NOTES

CAPTURE THE WORD	REFLECT ON THE MESSAGE	WALK IN FAITH

SERMON
NOTES

DATE:

SPEAKER   **TOPIC**

SCRIPTURE REFERENCE(S)

o

o

o

o

KEY POINTS

NOTES

CAPTURE THE WORD	REFLECT ON THE MESSAGE	WALK IN FAITH

SERMON NOTES

DATE:

SPEAKER   **TOPIC**

SCRIPTURE REFERENCE(S)

o

o

o

o

KEY POINTS

NOTES

_____
_____
_____
_____
_____
_____
_____
_____
_____
_____
_____
_____
_____
_____
_____
_____
_____

CAPTURE THE WORD	REFLECT ON THE MESSAGE	WALK IN FAITH

SERMON
NOTES

DATE:

SPEAKER   **TOPIC**

SCRIPTURE REFERENCE(S)

o

o

o

o

KEY POINTS

NOTES

CAPTURE THE WORD	REFLECT ON THE MESSAGE	WALK IN FAITH

This journal is designed to help you listen with purpose, write with clarity, and live with obedience. Each page is an invitation to draw nearer to God through His Word and to be transformed by it.

Capture the Word

"Write the vision; make it plain on tablets, so he may run who reads it." — *Habakkuk 2:2*

God's Word is living and active. As you take notes, you are preserving His truth so it can take root in your heart and guide your steps.

Reflect on the Message

"But his delight is in the law of the Lord, and on his law he meditates day and night." — *Psalm 1:2*

Reflection turns hearing into understanding. Meditating on scripture and sermons allows God's Word to shape your mind, renew your spirit, and deepen your walk.

Walk in Faith

"For we walk by faith, not by sight." — *2 Corinthians 5:7*
"But be doers of the word, and not hearers only, deceiving yourselves." — *James 1:22*

Faith grows when the Word is put into action. As you apply what you've written and reflected upon, you'll see God's promises unfold in your life.

May this journal be a faithful companion on your journey — reminding you to capture God's Word, reflect deeply on His truth, and walk daily in faith.